GIANT SEA REPTILES

OF THE DINOSAUR AGE

by CAROLINE ARNOLD

Illustrated by LAURIE CAPLE

Clarion Books
New York

To the memory of Dr. Elizabeth Nicholls, who was passionate
about fossils from childhood and whose dedication to paleontology
helped bring the world of prehistoric reptiles to life
—C.A.

For my sister Lynn Petroff—with fond memories
of childhood adventures with our lizards, Herman and Louie
—L.C.

The author and illustrator would like to thank Dr. Ryosuke Motani, Assistant Professor, Department of Geology, University of California, Davis, for his expert advice and reading of the manuscript. Also, Dr. Benjamin Kear, School of Earth and Environmental Sciences, University of Adelaide, Australia, for his careful attention.

Clarion Books
a Houghton Mifflin Company imprint
215 Park Avenue South, New York, NY 10003
Text copyright © 2007 by Caroline Arnold
Illustrations copyright © 2007 by Laurie Caple

The illustrations were executed in watercolor.
The text was set in 13-point Giovanni Book.

www.clarionbooks.com

Printed in Malaysia

Library of Congress Cataloging-in-Publication Data

Arnold, Caroline.
Giant sea reptiles of the dinosaur age / by Caroline Arnold ; illustrated by Laurie Caple.
p. cm.
Includes index.
ISBN 0-618-50449-4
1. Marine reptiles, Fossil—Juvenile literature. I. Caple, Laurie A., ill. II. Title.
QE861.A76 2007
567.9'37—dc22   2005014733

ISBN-13: 978-0-618-50449-7   ISBN-10: 0-618-50449-4

TWP 10 9 8 7 6 5 4 3 2

Marine reptile on cover: *Liopleurodon;* **marine reptile on title page:** *Plesiosaurus.*

Contents

Shonisaurus sikanniensis

An Ocean Giant

Two hundred and twenty million years ago, in waters that covered what is now western Canada, a huge marine reptile cruised the shallow seas. Propelling itself with flat, flipper-like limbs, the 70-foot (21-meter)-long animal hunted for shellfish and other small ocean animals, which it sucked into its long, toothless snout and swallowed. This fearsome creature was *Shonisaurus sikanniensis* (shon-ee-SAWR-uhs si-KAN-ee-EN-sis), a species of ichthyosaur (IK-thee-oh-SAWR), one of several types of large sea reptiles that inhabited the world's oceans in the Dinosaur Age.

The fossil remains of *Shonisaurus sikanniensis* were first discovered in 1991 when a hiker in northern British Columbia spotted some big fossil bones eroding out of the banks of the Sikanni Chief River. He reported his find to the Royal Tyrell Museum of Paleontology, in Drumheller, Alberta, where one of the curators, Dr. Elizabeth Nicholls, was an expert on pre-historic sea reptiles. She visited the site and was amazed by what she saw. The bones were bigger than those of any known marine reptile, and, incredibly, most of the skeleton was still intact. The only missing parts were the hind limbs. Over the course of three summers, the fossil skeleton was dug out of the ground and transported to the museum, where it was studied and pre-pared for exhibit. Every part of the animal proved to be huge. The massive skull weighed more than one and half tons, and the largest vertebrae, which measured nearly 11 inches (28 centimeters) across, were the size of dinner plates. In 2006, the giant skull of *Shonisaurus sikanniensis* went on display at the museum. Along with the rest of the skeleton, it will help answer questions about the appearance and lifestyle of this giant prehistoric predator and why it grew so big.

Rulers of Prehistoric Seas

Ichthyosaurs lived in the Mesozoic Era, a period between 250 and 65 million years ago, when reptiles were the dominant animals on Earth. During this time, the world was warmer than it is today, and there was no ice at the poles. The continents were closer together, and oceans covered much of the land. Two other groups of large reptiles also swam in Mesozoic seas—plesiosaurs (PLEE-see-oh-SAWRS) and mosasaurs (MOH-suh-sawrs). Ichthyosaurs, plesiosaurs, and mosasaurs are the largest marine reptiles ever known. We know about these giant predators from fossils of their bones, teeth, skin, and even the remains of the food they ate. Recent discoveries are helping us to learn more about their appearance, behavior, and other details of their lives.

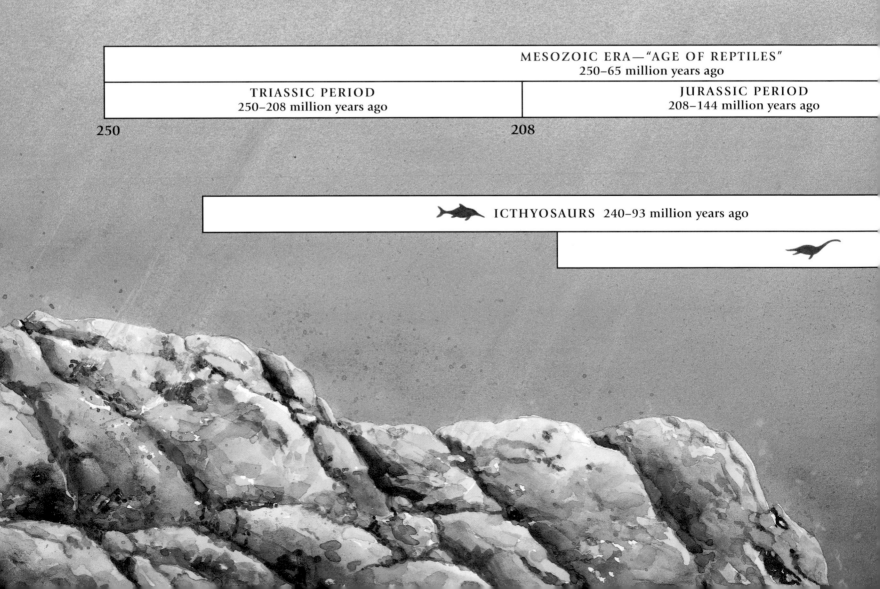

	MESOZOIC ERA—"AGE OF REPTILES" 250–65 million years ago	
TRIASSIC PERIOD 250–208 million years ago	JURASSIC PERIOD 208–144 million years ago

250   208

ICTHYOSAURS 240–93 million years ago

The Mesozoic Era is divided into three periods: the Triassic, about 250–208 million years ago; the Jurassic, about 208–144 million years ago; and the Cretaceous, about 144–65 million years ago. Ichthyosaurs first appeared in the Triassic, about 240 million years ago, and became extinct about 93 million years ago. Their bodies resembled those of present-day dolphins. The first plesiosaurs lived about 200 million years ago. Plesiosaurs and their relatives had varied forms, which included some species with extremely long necks and others with short necks and powerful, compact bodies. Mosasaurs appeared about 90 million years ago. They had sleek bodies, and they propelled themselves through the water with long flat tails. Both plesiosaurs and mosasaurs became extinct at the end of the Mesozoic Era.

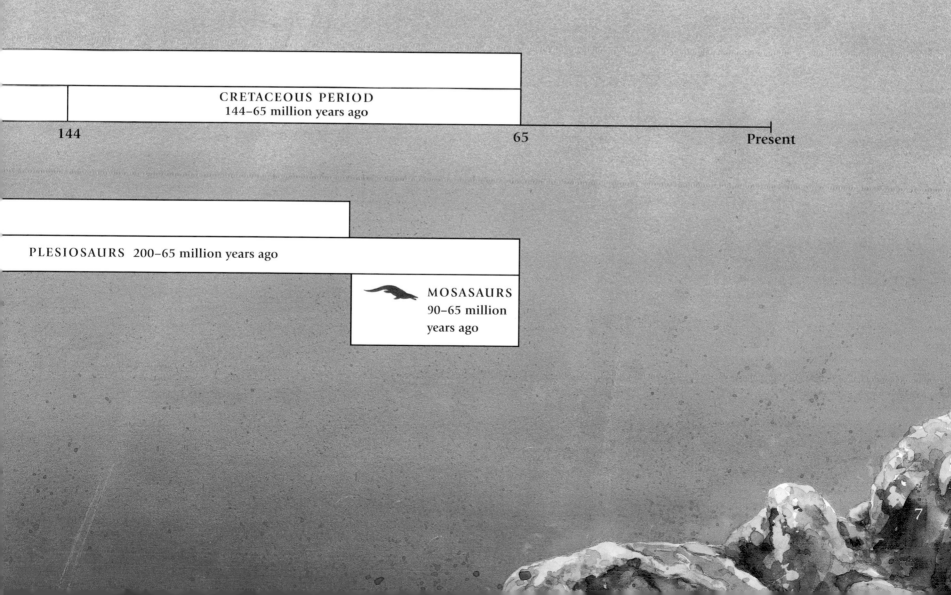

CRETACEOUS PERIOD
144–65 million years ago

144

65

Present

PLESIOSAURS 200–65 million years ago

MOSASAURS
90–65 million
years ago

7

Early Sea Reptiles

Smaller aquatic or semiaquatic reptiles that lived in the Mesozoic Era include nothosaurs (NO-tho-sawrs), placodonts (PLAK-oh-donts), turtles, and crocodiles. Nothosaurs and placodonts belonged to a large group of reptiles called sauropterygians (SAWR-oh-ter-IJ-ee-ans).

Nothosaurs

Nothosaurs are the earliest known aquatic reptiles and thrived in the Middle Triassic, about 230 million years ago. They were slender, long-necked fish eaters that ranged in size from a few inches to 13 feet (4 meters). They had streamlined bodies, long tails, and long necks with narrow heads. The edges of their mouths were lined with sharp, interlocking teeth, which they used to catch and trap fish. One of the most abundant species was *Nothosaurus mirabilis* (NO-tho-SAWR-us mih-RAB-ih-lis), which grew to be about 10 feet (3 meters) long. Fossils of two pregnant nothosaurs of a smaller species called *Keichosaurus* (KEE-cho-SAWR-us) were recently discovered in China. They show that nothosaurs did not lay eggs like most other reptiles but gave birth to live babies. Nothosaurs became extinct at the end of the Triassic Period, and their fossils have been found in Europe, Africa, and Asia.

Nothosaurus mirabilis

Armor-plated Swimmers

Placodonts were slow-moving, armor-plated aquatic reptiles. They lived during the Triassic, and their fossils have been found in Europe and the Middle East. They were relatively small, ranging in size from about 3 to 12 feet (.9 to 3.7 meters) in length. Placodonts had stout bodies and heavy bones, which helped them sink to the sea bottom. They fed on mollusks, which they crushed between large teeth on the roofs of their mouths and their lower jaws. Some species, such as *Placodus* (PLAK-oh-duhs), had shovel-like teeth protruding from the front of the snout as well. These may have been used to pry up shells from rocks and other hard surfaces. While some placodonts, such as *Placodus*, had armor plates only along their spines, other species were fully armored. One of these was *Henodus* (HEN-oh-duhs), whose broad, flattened body was covered with large plates, giving it a turtle-like appearance. *Henodus* lived in fresh water. It may have used its small teeth to filter tiny crustaceans from the water.

Placodus

Henodus

Ichthyosaurs

When the fossil bones of ichthyosaurs were first discovered in the early 1800s, people thought the strange animals seemed to be part fish and part reptile, which explains why they were given a name meaning "fish lizards." In fact, ichthyosaurs are not closely related to fish. Instead, their skeletons have characteristics similar to those of other reptiles.

The oldest known ichthyosaur, *Utatsusaurus* (oo-TA-tsu-SAWR-uhs), was 7 to 8 feet (2.1 to 2.4 meters) long and lived about 240 million years ago. Early ichthyosaurs were relatively small and had slender, lizard-like bodies. They probably swam with a side-to-side movement, like an eel or a catfish. Later ichthyosaurs had bigger, more compact bodies and vertical crescent-

Utatsusaurus

Stenopterygius

shaped tails, which they used to propel themselves through the water. Their limbs were large, flat paddles, which helped them steer and balance. The bones inside the paddles were packed in tight rows, which made them stiff. These larger, dolphin-like ichthyosaurs had bodies built for speed. Scientists calculate that the cruising speed of an 8.2-foot (2.5-meter)-long *Stenopterygius* (STEN-oh-ter-IJ-ee-uhs) was about 6 feet (1.8 meters) per second, about the same as a fast-swimming tuna. It is possible that, when swimming long distances or chasing prey, they leapt out of the water, much as dolphins and porpoises do today. In this way, an animal can go faster because it momentarily escapes the pull, or drag, of the water on its body.

Although reptiles typically have scaly skin, most fossil impressions of ichthyosaur skin show that it was smooth. Recently, however, an ichthyosaur fossil was found in a quarry near Solnhofen, in southern Germany, that appears to have tiny scales on one of its fins. It is from a species called *Aegirosaurus leptospondylus* (eye-GEER-oh-SAWR-uhs LEP-toe-SPOND-ee-luhs). Scientists are debating whether or not the marks actually represent scales.

A Seafood Diet

Ichthyosaurs cruised the oceans looking for food, sometimes diving to great depths. A favorite food of many ichthyosaurs were belemnites, ancient relatives of squid. Thousands of tiny fossilized hooks from belemnite tentacles have been found in the preserved stomach contents of ichthyosaurs, and also the remains of fish, crustaceans, and other sea animals. A recent examination of the stomach of a 110-million-year-old ichthyosaur fossil from Australia revealed the bones of fish, baby turtles, and even a small bird. We can also learn about the food that ichthyosaurs ate from fossils of other sea animals found in the same deposits as the ichthyosaur bones, and from coprolites, fossils of body waste.

One species of ichthyosaur that may have been a deep diver is *Opthalmosaurus* (off-THAL-moh-SAWR-uhs). Scientists estimate that it could dive to a depth of up to 2000 feet (610 meters) as it searched for squid and fish. This ichthyosaur may have been able to stay submerged for twenty minutes or more before coming back to the surface. Like reptiles that live on land, ichthyosaurs needed to breathe air. Their nostrils were located in front of their eyes.

Opthalmosaurus

Opthalmosaurus gets its name from its enormous eyes. In relation to the size of its body, they are the largest eyes of any animal ever known. A 15-foot (4.6-meter) animal had eyes 8 inches (20.3 centimeters) in diameter, the equivalent of a 6-foot (1.8-meter) human with eyes 4.5 inches (11.4 centimeters) across. The eyes were surrounded by a doughnut-shaped bone called the sclerotic ring. The biggest eyes of all belong to a larger relative, *Temnodontosaurus* (TEM-no-DONT-oh-SAWR-uhs), a species that grew to 30 feet (9.1 meters) long and had eyes nearly 10 inches (25.4 centimeters) across. Large eyes take in more light than small eyes and enable an animal to see more easily in dim ocean depths.

Baby Ichthyosaurs

Ichthyosaurs gave birth to live young. We know this because fossil skeletons of female ichthyosaurs have been found with bones of babies inside them. One female *Stenopterygius* had a body cavity in which seven embryos were preserved. The usual number of ichthyosaur babies a female had was two or three.

Some of the richest sources of mother-and-baby ichthyosaur fossils are the black-shale quarries at Holzmaden, near Stuttgart in southern Germany. Each year about thirty-five new ichthyosaur fossils are found there, and the total number discovered is about three thousand. Fossils of newborn baby ichthyosaurs at Holzmaden are between 20 and 34 inches (.5 and .9 meter) long. The unusual number of pregnant females found at this site suggests that females may have gathered there to give birth, much as some whales today go to sheltered coves to have their babies. About 185 million years ago, southern Germany was covered by a warm, shallow sea. When animals died, their bodies sank into a muddy ooze at the sea bottom. A lack of oxygen prevented decay, so bodies often remained intact as they fossilized; in some cases, impressions of soft tissues were preserved. They show the outlines of dorsal fins, fleshy pectoral fins, and fishlike tails.

Fossils of pregnant mosasaurs indicate that they, too, gave birth to live young. The position of the embryos suggests that the babies were born tail first. Although no fossils of pregnant plesiosaurs have been found, it is likely that their babies were also born alive.

Stenopterygius

15

Mary Anning, the Fossil Girl

One of the first ichthyosaur fossils was discovered in 1812 by a twelve-year-old girl, Mary Anning, near her home in Lyme Regis, on the southern coast of England. Fossil collecting was a popular hobby in the early 1800s, and Mary's family had a business collecting fossils and selling them to tourists. The nearby chalk cliffs were filled with the remains of marine animals that had lived 200 million years earlier, when this region was a shallow sea.

One day Mary's brother discovered the head of a huge reptilian-looking animal eroding out of the cliff face. He thought it was a crocodile. Later, after a fierce storm washed away more of the cliff, Mary found the neck and shoulders of the animal's skeleton. She and her brother excavated the bones and sold them to a fossil collector from London, who thought they belonged to a giant fish. At the time, little was known about prehistoric sea reptiles. It was not until several years later, after similar fossils had been found, that the skeleton was correctly identified as that of an ichthyosaur. Today it is on display at the British Museum in London, along with many more of Mary Anning's important finds.

In addition to her discoveries of at least three ichthyosaur skeletons, Mary Anning found fossils of two plesiosaurs and a pterodactyl, as well as numerous fish, ammonites (spiral-shelled mollusks that are ancient relatives of the chambered nautilus), brittle stars, and other marine animals, including many belemnites. Like squid, belemnites had ink sacs. One of the belemnites she found was complete with its fossil ink!

Although Mary Anning had little formal education, she had an uncanny knack for finding fossils and for understanding how the bones fit together. After excavating her specimens, she carefully reconstructed them and made detailed drawings. She collected fossils for many of the leading scientists of the day. Her work helped develop new ideas about what the world was like in prehistoric times.

Skeletons in the Desert

Until the recent discovery of the huge ichthyosaur in British Columbia, the largest known species was *Shonisaurus popularis* (shon-ee-SAWR-uhs POP-yew-LAR-uhs), whose fossil remains are preserved in the Nevada desert in Berlin-Ichthyosaur State Park. *Shonisaurus* gets its name from the mountains of the Shoshone Range that surround the site. About 230 million years ago, this region was covered by a tropical sea. It became a watery graveyard for at least forty ichthyosaurs, including some individuals that are 50 feet (15.2 meters) long. In life, the animals may have weighed up to 40 tons (36,287 kilograms). Most of the fossil skeletons are nearly complete, allowing scientists to get a clear picture of what these animals looked like. The largest individuals had fins that were 6 feet (1.8 meters) long, and tails that were 25 feet (7.6 meters) long. Their skulls were 10 feet (3 meters) long and were filled with two hundred sharp, cone-shaped teeth, which were ideal for grasping fish and ammonites. Fossils of ammonites are also embedded in the stone.

The fossil bones of *Shonisaurus* were first dug out by miners who came to Nevada in the late 1800s. The miners decorated their cabins with the fossils, and in some cases used the huge *Shonisaurus* vertebrae as dinner plates! In a living ichthyosaur, the disk-shaped vertebrae were packed tightly together, like a stack of giant checkers. This arrangement made the spine stiff and strong. The first scientific excavations began in 1954. Today, visitors to the state park can see some of the remaining fossil skeletons still in the ground and appreciate how enormous these animals were. *Shonisaurus* is the Nevada state fossil.

Shonisaurus popularis

Ammonites

19

Plesiosaurs

When the first plesiosaur fossils were found in the early 1800s, people thought the bones of these reptiles looked more lizard-like than those of the recently discovered ichthyosaurs. So they gave them the name "plesiosaur," meaning "near lizard," reflecting the belief that they were nearer, or more closely related, to lizards. In fact, the plesiosaurs are part of the same large group of aquatic reptiles as nothosaurs and placodonts, the sauropterygians. Fossils of plesiosaurs have been found on every continent of the world, including Antarctica.

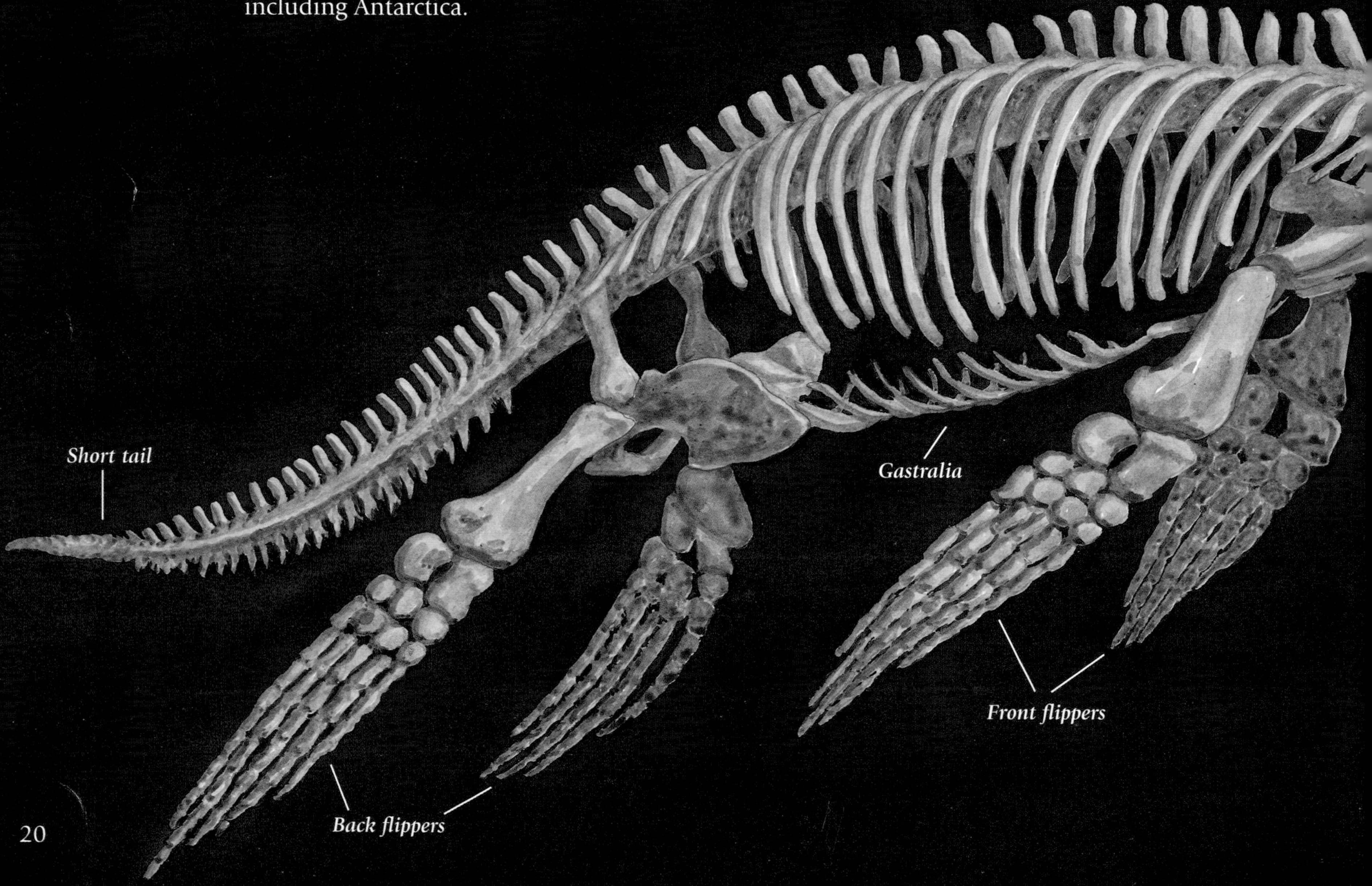

Short tail

Gastralia

Front flippers

Back flippers

Long neck

Small head

There were many different kinds of plesiosaurs, ranging from species with small heads and long necks, such as *Plesiosaurus* (PLEE-see-oh-SAWR-uhs), to those with large heads and short necks, such as *Pliosaurus* (PLIE-oh-SAWR-uhs). Scientists continue to work on classifying all the different kinds of plesiosaurs and finding out how they are related to one another.

The central portion of a plesiosaur's body was supported by the ribs, which were connected to the spine, as well as by a series of bones, called gastralia, that extended across the lower body between the bones of the chest and the pelvis. Muscles attached to the gastralia may have been used to expand the body cavity when breathing. Gastralia may also have helped stiffen the body, which would have made it easier for the animal to move through the water while swimming. Ichthyosaur skeletons also have gastralia, but those of mosasaurs do not. Plesiosaurs propelled themselves through the water with broad, flat limbs, moving them up and down, much as a bird flaps its wings.

Long Necks

The first well-preserved plesiosaur skeleton was excavated by Mary Anning at Lyme Regis in 1824. The 7.5-foot (2.3-meter)-long fossil was of an animal with a small head, a thin neck, four long, paddle-like flippers, and a tapered body ending in a short tail. In life, it would have weighed about 200 pounds (91 kilograms). It lived about 200 million years ago, in the early Jurassic. It was named *Plesiosaurus dolichodeirus* (PLEE-see-oh-SAWR-uhs DOL-ik-oh-DIE-ruhs), meaning "long-necked plesiosaur."

All of the long-necked plesiosaurs had short, round bodies and slender necks and tails. Their shape has been described like that of a snake threaded through the body of a turtle. Scientists usually divide the long-necked plesiosaurs into three groups: the plesiosaurids (PLEE-see-oh-SAWR-ids), the cryptoclitids (KRIP-toe-KLIE-tids), and the elasmosaurs (ee-LAS-mo-SAWRS). The plesiosaurids, such as *Plesiosaurus dolichodeirus*, were the earliest of these, and all of the other plesiosaurs are thought to have descended from them.

Plesiosaurus dolichodeirus

Dimorphodon

23

Elasmosaurus

The elasmosaurs were large animals with unusually long necks, with the longest of all belonging to *Elasmosaurus* (ee-LAS-mo-SAWR-uhs). Its neck grew up to a length of 23 feet (7 meters) and had as many as seventy-two vertebrae, the most neck vertebrae of any known animal. A full-grown *Elasmosaurus* could have a total body length of up to 46 feet (14 meters) and weigh more than 11 tons (9979 kilograms). The elasmosaurs probably used their flexible necks to reach out and snatch fish or other food. Their thin, sharp teeth would have been good for grasping and holding prey.

The cryptoclitids had somewhat shorter necks than the elasmosaurs. Their broad, short skulls had jaws filled with thin, interlocking teeth, which were good for trapping small, soft-bodied prey such as fish and crustaceans. A typical species was *Cryptoclidus* (KRIP-toe-KLIE-duhs). It grew between 10 and 13 feet (3 and 4 meters) long. Its fossil bones have been found in southern England.

Cryptoclidus

Ferocious Predators

Plesiosaurs with short necks first appeared about 200 million years ago and died out about 80 million years ago. They were ferocious predators with powerful bodies, big heads, and large jaws filled with dagger-like teeth. They preyed on smaller plesiosaurs, ichthyosaurs, crocodiles, turtles, fish, and ammonites. All of the reptiles in this group used to be called pliosaurs. Now, however, scientists think that the various species may have several different origins, and they no longer group them together under this name.

Kronosaurus

Notochelone

Many of the short-necked plesiosaurs were very large. *Kronosaurus* (KRO-no-SAWR-uhs) was a massive animal 35 feet (10.7 meters) long with a 9-foot (2.7-meter)-long skull. Its fossil teeth and bones have been found in Queensland, Australia. A species that may have grown as long as 50 feet (15.2 meters) is *Liopleurodon* (LIE-oh-PLOOR-oh-don). The skull of this giant is more than a quarter of its total body length, and its huge jaws are lined with large, sharp teeth. Fossils of *Liopleurodon* have been found in England, France, Germany, and Russia. A recent discovery of a short-necked plesiosaur in northwestern Mexico may be of an animal that was up to 45 feet (13.7 meters) long. It has been dubbed the "Monster of Aramberri" after the village near the fossil site. The skeleton is in the process of being excavated and studied. It is unique both for its size and for being the first such fossil from that part of the world.

The short-necked plesiosaurs were larger than most other marine predators of the time. After the ichthyosaurs died out, about 93 million years ago, the short-necked plesiosaurs became the top predators of the ocean.

America's Inland Sea

During the late Cretaceous Period, the center of the North American continent was covered by a vast, shallow sea known as the Western Interior Seaway. The levels and boundaries shifted constantly, and at times, it was so large that its waters connected the Gulf of Mexico and the Arctic Ocean. Gradually, this sea dried up, leaving behind the fossilized remains of its inhabitants. From the southern United States to northern Canada, scientists have unearthed thousands of fossil bones belonging to plesiosaurs, mosasaurs, and many other animals that once swam in these ancient waters.

Western Interior Seaway, about 100 million years ago

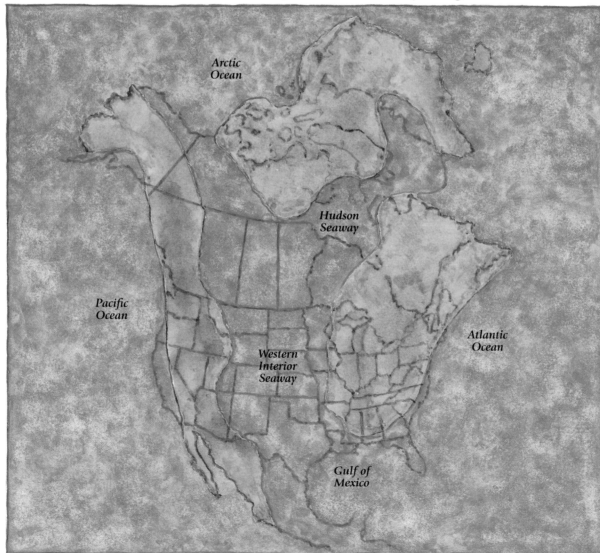

A Fossil Mistake

In 1867, Dr. Edward Cope, a scientist and fossil collector in Philadelphia at the Academy of Natural Sciences, received a package in the mail. In it were three huge vertebrae found by an amateur fossil hunter near his home in central Kansas. The bones were intriguing, so Dr. Cope asked the sender to dig out the rest of the animal's skeleton and ship it to him. When the 900 pounds (408 kilograms) of bones arrived, Dr. Cope examined them and determined that they belonged to a new kind of plesiosaur. He named it *Elasmosaurus platyurus* (ee-LAS-mo-SAWR-uhs plat-ee-YOOR-uhs), meaning "plate lizard with a flat tail," after the large, plate-like bones on the underside of the body and what he mistakenly thought was a long, flat tail. As it turned out, the tail was actually an extremely long neck! After Dr. Cope assembled the 40-foot (12.2-meter) skeleton, a rival scientist visited the museum and pointed out the error. Dr. Cope quickly changed the head to the other end of the skeleton. Unfortunately, he had already published a paper describing his new discovery, so to his embarrassment, his mistake became public knowledge.

Elasmosaurus platyurus

29

Stomach Stones

Styxosaurus (STIK-SO-SAWR-uhs) was another large, long-necked plesiosaur that lived in North America's ancient inland sea. This reptile grew to a length of more than 30 feet (9.1 meters), and its neck contained sixty-two vertebrae. In one fossil skeleton of a *Styxosaurus*, recently excavated in Logan County, Kansas, the body cavity contained fish bones and scales—the remains of the animal's last meal—as well as ninety-five smooth, rounded stones. The largest stone weighed nearly a pound. Such stones, found within the digestive system of an animal, are called gastroliths. Some plesiosaur skeletons have as many as a thousand gastroliths associated with them.

It may be that gastroliths helped plesiosaurs "chew" their food in the same way that present-day birds and crocodiles swallow pebbles to help break up their food so that it can be digested more easily. (Birds have no teeth, and crocodiles have no chewing teeth.) Another possibility is that gastroliths served as ballast to assist the plesiosaurs in balancing their bodies while swimming, although this seems unlikely since the total weight of the stones was small compared with the enormous weight of these huge animals. It may be that plesiosaurs ate stones for their mineral content—or perhaps swallowed them by accident. No one knows for sure. Gastroliths are also associated with the fossil skeletons of dinosaurs.

Plesiosaur gastroliths are typically hard rock such as granite, quartzite, or basalt. Some are highly polished, while others have dull or waxy surfaces. Plesiosaurs would have picked up these stones from the sea floor. Since mineral deposits vary from place to place, the composition of the stones helps identify their origin and provides information about where plesiosaurs roamed.

Styxosaurus

31

Mosasaurs

Mosasaurs first appeared about 90 million years ago, in the middle of the Cretaceous Period. When short-necked plesiosaurs became extinct about 80 million years ago, mosasaurs replaced them as the supreme predators of the sea. Mosasaurs are distant relatives of present-day monitor lizards such as the Komodo dragon. Preserved impressions of mosasaur skin show that it was made of smooth, diamond-shaped scales.

Globidens

Ammonites

Mosasaurs were the first giant sea reptiles to be discovered. In 1780, workers in a limestone mine in the Netherlands came upon a huge fossilized skeleton. The jaw was more than 5 feet (1.5 meters) long and lined with powerful, backward-curving teeth. In life, the animal would have been 58 feet (17.7 meters) long and have weighed about 20 tons (18,144 kilograms). At first, people thought that the bones belonged to a whale; only later did they recognize them as being from a reptile. The animal was given the name "mosasaur," meaning "Meuse lizard," after the Meuse River, which flows near the mine. Although many other mosasaurs have since been discovered, this specimen is still the largest one that has ever been found. It is now on display at the National Museum of Natural History in Paris.

Fossils of mosasaurs have been found all over the world, including Antarctica. More than twenty species of mosasaurs are known. Although most of them were ferocious predators, one group, which includes a species called *Globidens* (GLO-bee-denz), had ball-shaped teeth adapted for crushing hard-shelled animals such as ammonites.

Top Predators

Mosasaurs were the top predators in North America's inland sea, and their fossils are especially numerous in Kansas and South Dakota, where more than 1800 specimens have been found. The largest known species is *Tylosaurus* (TIE-lo-SAWR-uhs). This reptile could grow as long as 50 feet (15.2 meters) and weigh up to 11 tons (9979 kilograms). Mosasaurs like *Tylosaurus* grabbed prey in their long jaws, using their cone-shaped teeth to hold it tight. A flexible hinge on the lower jaw allowed the mosasaur to open wide and swallow its food whole or in large pieces. The blunt tip of *Tylosaurus*'s jaw projected beyond the front teeth. The giant reptile may have used the front of its jaw as a ram to stun its prey or to defend itself against other predators.

Mosasaurs were excellent swimmers and propelled themselves through the water with a side-to-side motion of their long tails. Most of them ambushed their prey, making a swift attack and catching it by surprise. They probably ate anything they could find, including other mosasaurs. The preserved stomach contents of a *Tylosaurus* found in South Dakota contains the remains of a smaller mosasaur, a bird, a fish, and what may have been a shark.

Tylosaurus

Clidastes

35

The End of the Dinosaur Age

While ichthyosaurs disappeared from the Earth's oceans about 93 million years ago, some plesiosaurs and mosasaurs lived to the end of the Mesozoic Era, 65 million years ago. Then they too became extinct, along with all the dinosaurs, winged reptiles called pterosaurs, and many other species. Ichthyosaurs, plesiosaurs, and mosasaurs were the largest reptiles ever known to swim the Earth's oceans. They are part of the amazing diversity of life in the Dinosaur Age. As we continue to learn about these huge marine reptiles and their prehistoric ocean environment, we gain a better understanding of what the world was like when they were alive.

Ichthyosaurs, plesiosaurs, and mosasaurs were real-life monsters that dominated the seas for 150 million years. They were fearsome and fascinating predators. With sharp teeth, quick reflexes, and bodies adapted to life in the water, these giant reptiles were the supreme rulers of ancient seas. Today, as we look at their fossilized teeth and bones, we can only imagine the terror they must have struck in the lives of other ocean inhabitants many millions of years ago.

Where You Can See Fossils of Ancient Sea Reptiles

Fossils of ichthyosaurs, plesiosaurs, and mosasaurs are displayed in many museums. Here are some of the places in North America where you can see fossils and learn about these prehistoric sea reptiles:

The United States

Academy of Natural Sciences, Philadelphia, Pennsylvania

American Museum of Natural History, New York, New York

Berlin-Ichthyosaur State Park, Austin, Nevada

Denver Museum of Nature and Science, Denver, Colorado

Field Museum, Chicago, Illinois

Johnston Geology Museum, Emporia State University, Emporia, Kansas

Museum of Comparative Zoology, Harvard University, Cambridge, Massachusetts

Museum of Geology, South Dakota School of Mines and Technology,
    Rapid City, South Dakota

Museum of the Rockies, Montana State University, Bozeman, Montana

National Museum of Natural History, Smithsonian Institution, Washington, D.C.

Natural History Museum of Los Angeles County, Los Angeles, California

North Dakota Heritage Center, Pembina State Museum, Bismarck, North Dakota

Peabody Museum of Natural History, Yale University, New Haven, Connecticut

Sternberg Museum of Natural History, Fort Hays State University, Fort Hays, Kansas

Texas Memorial Museum, University of Texas, Austin, Texas

University of Wisconsin, Geology Museum, Madison, Wisconsin

University of Wyoming Geological Museum, Laramie, Wyoming

Canada

National Museum of Natural Sciences, Ottawa, Ontario

Royal Ontario Museum, Toronto, Ontario

Royal Tyrell Museum, Drumheller, Alberta

Index